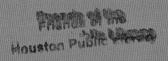

The My Encyclopedia Collection

My Encyclopedia of Baby Animals
My Encyclopedia of the Forest
My Encyclopedia of Insects and Bugs
My Encyclopedia of the Sea

Library of Congress Cataloging-in-Publication Data

Names: Figueras, Emmanuelle.
Title: My encyclopedia of baby animals / by Emmanuelle Figueras ; translated by Joy Nevin Axelson.
Other titles: Mon encyclo des bebes animaux. English
Description: New York, NY : Children's Press, 2016. | Includes bibliographical references and index.
Identifiers: LCCN 2016005791| ISBN 9780531224717 (library binding : alk. paper) | ISBN 9780531225950 (hardcover : alk. paper)
Subjects: LCSH: Animals--Infancy--Encyclopedias, Juvenile. | Animals--Infancy--Juvenile literature.
Classification: LCC QL763 .F54213 2016 | DDC 591.3/92--dc23 LC record available at http://lccn.loc.gov/2016005791

Produced by Spooky Cheetah Press
Translation by Joy Nevin Axelson

Mon encyclo des bébés animaux © Editions Milan 2009
Translation © 2017 Scholastic Inc.

Printed in China 62

My encyclopedia of baby animals

Emmanuelle Figueras

Table of Contents

Happy Birthday

Not all animals are born the same way. Some grow inside their mothers' bellies before being born. Others develop outside their mothers' bodies—inside an egg or a pouch. Let's discover them together!

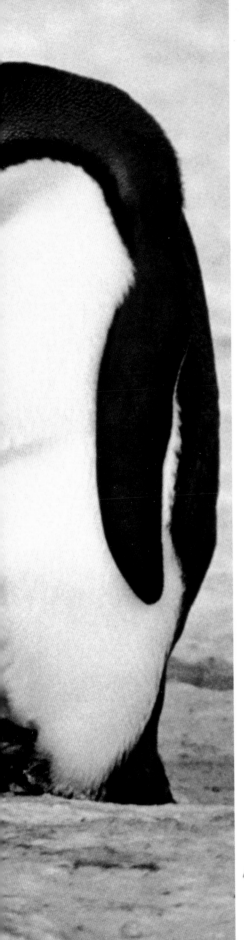

Inside Mommy's Belly

Mammal babies develop inside their mothers' bodies. After they are born, they drink their mothers' milk.

The Wildebeest

All baby wildebeests on the African savanna look alike. But within the herd, each mom recognizes her own baby by its scent.

Wildebeests are born almost fully developed. Within minutes after its birth, this baby will be able to walk!

The Gazelle

A female gazelle separates herself from the herd to give birth to her young. Her baby comes out very quickly. ...It is all wet! The mother licks her baby to dry it off and to make sure it is healthy.

Soon after cleaning her baby, the mother gazelle will leave it alone. The fawn stays hidden to keep safe from predators.

The Elephant

You spend about nine months developing in your mother's belly. Baby elephants take more than twice that long! After a baby elephant is born, all the adult elephants in the herd will help care for it.

Soon after it is born, a baby elephant's female relatives help clean it.

The Sea Lion

Like dolphins and whales, sea lions are marine mammals. Although they give birth on land, sea lions spend a lot of their time in the water. Before long, a mother sea lion will bring her baby swimming with her.

A sea lion gives birth to a pup.

The Donkey

A baby donkey is rolled up in a ball as it grows inside its mother's belly. When it is being born, the donkey's front hooves come out first. Then its little body unfolds. About half an hour later, the foal is out and on the ground!

From the moment it is born, a donkey foal tries to stand up so it can drink milk from its mother.

Daddy Daycare

Do you know what an emperor penguin, a midwife toad, and a sea dragon have in common? Dads are the ones who bring their babies into the world!

Midwife toads carry their eggs for several weeks.

The Midwife Toad

This animal has a strange way of making babies! The female lays her eggs on the male's back legs. He protects them until they hatch.

The Emperor Penguin

A female emperor penguin lays a single egg and transfers it to her mate. Then she heads to the sea to hunt. The male emperor goes without eating as he takes care of the egg. He will protect it until the female returns—about two months later.

To keep his egg from freezing, this penguin must always keep it wedged between his tummy and his feet.

The sea dragon is a little fish that lives off the southern and eastern coasts of Australia.

The Sea Dragon

A female sea dragon deposits her eggs under a male's tail. He carries them until they are ready to hatch. Then he releases the eggs into the water.

The Cardinal Fish

This fish takes the prize for most bizarre! The male incubates the female's eggs in his mouth. No predators can find them there!

A cardinal fish keeps his eggs safe until they hatch.

Water Babies

Splish, splash! ...Animals who live in the sea are born underwater. Luckily, all of these babies know how to swim right away.

The Dolphin

Look! A mama dolphin is giving birth to her baby underwater. Dolphins are mammals—they need to breathe air. As soon as a dolphin is born, its mother and another adult help it to the surface to take a big breath!

A baby dolphin is called a calf. It will stay by its mother's side for up to six years.

The Dogfish

The dogfish is a type of shark. Like all fish, it can breathe well underwater. A baby dogfish grows inside a strange-looking egg case. Mom attaches the egg case to algae so it won't float away on ocean currents.

The dogfish spends between five and 11 months in its egg case, hidden among the algae.

The grunion lives in the ocean off the coast of California.

The Grunion

This little fish comes out of the water to lay thousands of eggs on the beach. The eggs hatch after they are swept out to sea.

The Octopus

The octopus is a mollusk that has a soft body and no bones. Some species of octopus have thousands of brothers and sisters! They come from eggs that their mother lays in a hole in a large rock.

The mother octopus stays with her eggs until they are ready to hatch. Soon after that, she dies.

An Eggcellent Start

Many baby animals grow inside an egg.
They are called oviparous. When the animals are fully
developed, they are ready to break out of their shells.

The Ostrich

Ccrrrackk! Enormous eggs break open and several little heads appear among the shells. A baby ostrich uses the hardest part of its beak to break out of its egg.

Baby ostriches are able to walk soon after hatching. Even though they are birds, ostriches will never be able to fly.

The Green Lizard

Like most reptiles, the green lizard is oviparous. It hatches from an egg. Some of its reptile cousins, like the boa constrictor, give birth to live young. Those animals are viviparous.

Baby lizards grow for about three months in their eggs before hatching.

Grass snakes' eggs have soft shells.

The Grass Snake

A baby grass snake uses its egg tooth to chip away at its shell when it is ready to hatch. The snake loses the tooth shortly afterward. Once her baby hatches, the mother snake can finally leave to hunt frogs, toads, and newts.

The Red Kite

How cute! After spending about one month well protected in their eggs, red kite babies are ready to hatch. The chicks are born with their fluffy feathers all ruffled.

Two little red kites have broken out of their eggs. The third should hatch soon.

Strange Snail Tales

Most of the time, two parents are needed to make a baby—a male and a female. The land snail, however, is a special case: Moms can also be dads!

Are You My Mom?

Land snails are hermaphroditic. That means a snail can be both male and female at the same time. Isn't that amazing?

When two snails mate, both usually carry the fertilized eggs.

Snails grow next to about 100 of their brothers and sisters. Each one has its own little egg that is round like a marble.

A baby snail has a very fragile shell—it is see-through and very soft. The newly hatched snail will eat its egg to get the calcium needed to build up its shell.

Inside the Pocket

Have you ever heard of a marsupial? These babies grow inside a fur pouch on their mothers' bellies.

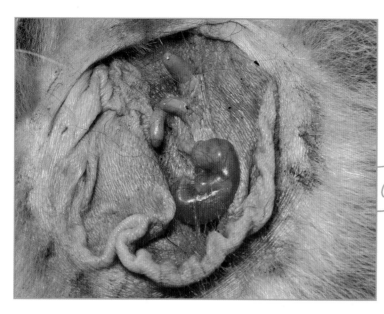

The Red-Necked Wallaby

A little wallaby is born completely naked and blind. It must quickly take shelter in its mother's pouch to stay warm and safe from danger.

Right after it is born, the little wallaby crawls through its mom's fur to her pouch.

Inside the mama's pouch, a baby brushtail never lets go of its free milk supply.

The Brushtail Possum

Like almost all other marsupials, brushtail possums live in Australia. They live high up in the trees. Brushtails are nocturnal. So they spend most of the day asleep.

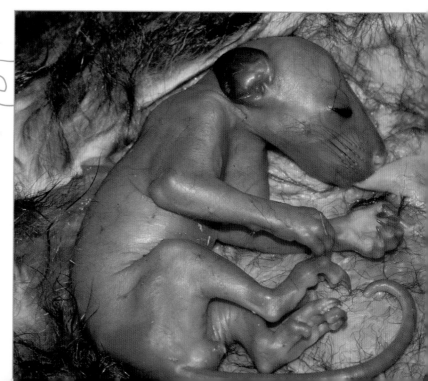

The Koala

A koala spends the first six or seven months of its life in its mother's pouch. There it finds everything it needs to grow: warmth, protection, and its mother's milk.

Koalas are often referred to as koala bears, but they are not really bears at all!

This baby kangaroo is peeking out of its mother's pouch to look at the world. If the youngster sees anything dangerous, it pops right back in!

The Red Kangaroo

A newborn red kangaroo is no bigger than your thumb. And it looks like a big pink bean! Right after birth, it quickly crawls toward its mother's pouch to continue growing where it is warm.

Funny Babies

Look closely. ...Many baby animals look very different from what they will look like as adults. They are often tiny, very fragile—and kind of clumsy!

In Their Birthday Suits

Many animals are born naked.
They start to grow their fur or feathers later.

The Rabbit

Rabbits are born naked and blind. A baby bunny cuddles up to its brothers and sisters to stay warm in the cozy nest their mother made. The baby is so small that it weighs less than an orange!

Baby rabbits are called kits or kittens. They often have many siblings.

The Kingfisher

What a funny bird! At birth, baby kingfishers have round tummies and no feathers. Their eyes are stuck shut, so they can't see anything at all.

Baby kingfishers eat fish that their parents bring to them.

No one would dare to bother this baby crocodile when it is sitting between its mom's sharp teeth!

The Nile Crocodile

A crocodile digs a hole and lays her eggs inside. Just before hatching, the babies start to make high-pitched calls. Mama croc digs up the nest and carries her babies in her mouth to the water.

The Crab

A baby crab is very small and soft. This cute crustacean will make about 10 shells for itself before it has a really hard shell like an adult crab's.

This baby crab is so small, it can fit in the palm of a hand.

Whose Baby Is This?

Can you tell whose babies these are?
Many baby animals don't look at all like
their parents. They change as they mature.

Young wild boars are called piglets.
You can recognize them by their stripes.

The Wild Boar

Baby boars are very different from
their parents. As they grow, their hair
turns from orange to dark brown.
The boars will become much
tougher—and a lot less cute!

The Cheetah

A baby cheetah is born with a tall strip of
hair that runs down its back. This mantle
makes the cub look like an aggressive animal
called a honey badger and helps keep
predators away. The mantle starts to disappear
around the time the cub is three months old.

This baby cheetah lives far from
here on the African savanna.

The Raccoon

Baby raccoons are called kits. They are often born in well-hidden forest dens. Their coats and masks look different from those of their parents.

Baby raccoons have lighter-colored masks than their parents'.

The Deer

Until they are about four months old, fawns have white spots all over their backs. They look like they have been splattered with white paint!

A baby deer is called a fawn. An adult male is called a buck, and an adult female is a doe.

The Swan

Baby swans are called cygnets. They are covered in fluffy gray down that will soon be replaced by beautiful white feathers. Their gray beaks will become a lovely shade of orange.

Next to their mother, these cygnets look like baby ducks.

First Steps

On your mark, get set, go! Some animals scamper along behind their mothers right after birth. These little ones can't hang around when danger is lurking nearby.

This giraffe calf is not sure of itself yet, but its mom encourages it to follow her.

The Giraffe

Baby giraffes are called calves. When they are born, they fall six feet (1.8 meters) to the ground! The calves get up almost right away. They have to be ready to run from lions looking for lunch on the savanna.

Ducklings follow one another in a line so they won't get lost.

The Duck

Quack! Quack! Immediately after hatching, ducklings call to their mother. Whew! There she is. Soon the whole group waddles toward the pond.

Baby llamas look fragile. However, they know how to gallop the day they are born.

The Llama

Less than one hour after being born, a baby llama can stand. Even though its legs are a little wobbly, it can still follow along behind its mother.

The Reindeer

Reindeer can walk the day they are born. Mother and baby must quickly rejoin their herd so the baby reindeer will be safe among the adults.

If it does not stay with the herd, this little reindeer could get attacked by wolves.

From Tadpole to Frog

Tadpoles do not look at all like their parents. Their bodies change gradually until they transform into frogs.

Eggs in the Pond

Most frogs lay their eggs in water. They may lay thousands of eggs at a time! Soon tiny tadpoles emerge. They have round bodies, long tails, and no legs.

Tadpoles live in the water, where they feed on algae. The tadpoles grow quickly. After about six weeks, they start to grow tiny legs.

This tadpole has grown legs. Soon it will lose its tail and look like a frog.

Can you believe a tadpole
turned into this frog?
Now it can feel equally at
home in water or on land.

From Egg to Butterfly

You probably know that caterpillars turn into butterflies. But do you know how they do it? The story of metamorphosis is interesting indeed....

Butterflies lay tiny eggs with growing babies inside. Each species of butterfly lays its eggs on a carefully chosen plant. This is what its baby will eat once it hatches.

A Large Appetite

After hatching, a baby butterfly pigs out! It stuffs itself with so many leaves that it becomes a plump caterpillar. Then, when it is big enough, the caterpillar stops eating and focuses on metamorphosis. Now it will undergo the major change that turns it into a butterfly.

The caterpillar forms itself into a chrysalis. Inside it is changing into a butterfly!

Something is moving on that twig. ...It's
a butterfly coming out of its chrysalis!
This caterpillar turned into a magnificent
black-veined white butterfly!

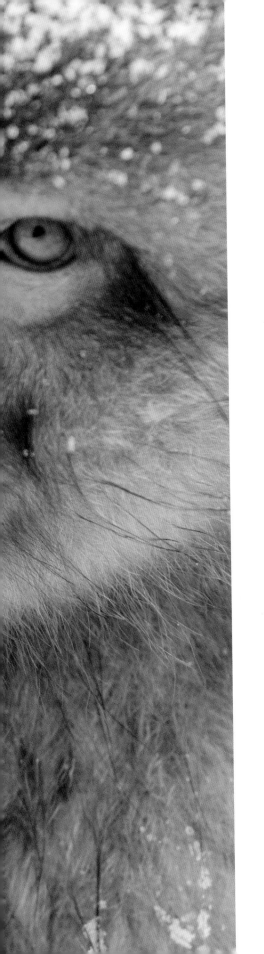

Family Life

Everybody's different!
Some baby animals are raised by
their mothers or by their entire
families. Others are on their
own from their first day of life.

Watchful Mothers

These animals do best when they stay with their mothers. Whether riding on Mom's back or holding tightly to her fur, these babies stay safe from harm.

The Giant Panda

Giant panda cubs are raised by their mothers in the forests of China. The little bear will follow its mom everywhere until it is at least one and a half years old.

This giant panda baby may look sturdy and tough, but it still really likes hugs!

The Pangolin

What a strange baby! At birth, the pangolin has soft scales. Its scales only begin to harden two days later.

At one month old, the baby pangolin is ready to leave the burrow. It rides on its mom's tail as she forages for termites.

The Horse

Baby horses are called foals. From the moment they are born, they are very attached to their mothers. Male foals are called colts. Female foals are called fillies.

This foal and its mom are inseparable.

The Wolf Spider

Not many animals would dare attack baby wolf spiders! Their mother keeps them with her until they are big enough to survive on their own.

A mother wolf spider protects her young by carrying them on her back.

The Anteater

You can easily recognize an anteater by its long nose. Baby anteaters live with their mothers until they are two years old. Together, they attack and feast on up to 30,000 ants and termites each day.

Baby anteaters often ride on their mothers' backs. Their large claws help them hang on to their mothers' fur.

Taking Turns

Gibbons and terns are just two animals that are raised by both of their parents. The male and the female take turns caring for their young.

The Gibbon

A shadow is swinging through the trees. ...It's a gibbon! It can easily be recognized by its long arms. This acrobatic monkey lives in the forests of Asia.

This little gibbon will live with its parents until it is about six years old.

The Lion

Lions are the only big cats that live in groups, called prides. The male does his part in caring for the young by protecting the entire pride from enemies.

This ferocious lion can be very gentle with his cubs.

The Tern

How exhausting! These birds must catch many fish to feed their little ones, who are constantly clamoring for food.

Tern parents, like other bird species, take turns feeding their young.

Nurseries and Nannies

Some animals take teamwork to a whole new level!
Other adults in the group watch the babies
when their parents are away.

Baby sperm whales are never left alone.

The Sperm Whale

Although it already weighs as much as a rhino, this baby sperm whale cannot defend itself against a great white shark. When its mother is off hunting, the rest of the pod protects the baby.

"Halt! Who goes there?" Meerkats keep a close eye out for danger.

The Meerkat

What a funny animal! The meerkat is a small South African mongoose. Several meerkat families live together in a group, called a gang or a mob. Within the group, all the adults take care of the babies, called pups.

Female bats often form large groups to raise their pups together.

The Bat

Bats may look scary, but they pose little threat to humans. Bats are small flying mammals. They come out at night to hunt. They sleep hanging upside down during the day.

The Pink Flamingo

These magnificent birds love to wade in the water. There they feed on tiny shrimp, which contain chemicals that give the birds their beautiful pink plumage.

They can't fly yet, so baby flamingos count on the adults to keep them safe.

On Their Own

Did you know that many insects, reptiles, and amphibians do not need parents to raise them?

The Grasshopper

In spring, a grasshopper hatches from an egg. The baby, called a nymph, looks just like an adult grasshopper without wings.

Grasshoppers escape from their enemies by hiding in the grass.

Hermann's Tortoise

Like many reptiles, this baby tortoise developed in an egg hidden in the sand. It hatched at the end of summer and quickly began hunting insects and snails.

Once out of the shell, this baby tortoise is on its own to find food.

This newly hatched snail is hungry! It starts eating right away.

The Snail
Although it may have 100 siblings, a baby snail is on its own after birth.

The Dogfish
During the day, the dogfish hides itself on the ocean floor. It only ventures out at night to catch small fish and crustaceans.

In the ocean, this baby dogfish learns right away how to survive on its own.

An Odd Bird

The cuckoo bird is unique in the animal world.
Some females lay their eggs in other birds' nests.
The adoptive mothers raise the cuckoo chicks as their own.

Tricky Bird

A female cuckoo abandons her egg in the nest of a robin or warbler. Then she removes one of the eggs that was already there so the nest will still contain the same number of eggs.

This baby cuckoo is always hungry. He anxiously awaits the return of his adoptive parents, who are out getting food for him.

The cuckoo's main goal is to quickly get rid of any other eggs in the nest—so there are fewer mouths to feed!

Whoa! As it grows, it becomes clear that the baby cuckoo is much bigger than its adoptive parent.

Dinner Is Served!

Flower petals, caterpillars, ants, raw fish, grass—baby animals eat food that is very different from what is on your plate!

Yum! Warm Milk

Mammals drink their mothers' milk before they begin to eat plants or meat.

The Pig

Baby pigs are called piglets and often have more than 10 siblings. Fortunately, the mama pig usually has a separate spot for each piglet to drink from!

Look out! Piglets will shove each other out of the way to get to the teat with the most milk.

The Camel

A baby camel will drink its mother's milk for about a year. Then, since camels are herbivores, the youngster will start to eat the plants and grasses it finds in the desert.

This baby camel got to its feet right after it was born. Then it could drink its mother's milk standing up!

The Bonobo

The bonobo is a close relative of the chimpanzee. It lives in the Democratic Republic of Congo in Africa. Like all mammals, bonobos drink their mothers' milk for both nourishment and for reassurance when they are a little upset.

If a baby bonobo has any trouble nursing, its mom will help immediately.

Grass and Leaves

Herbivores are animals that eat only plants.
They have big appetites!

The Bison

On the prairie there is grass everywhere so animals can just lower their heads to eat. The bigger the animals get, the more they eat. An adult bison eats about 30 pounds (13 kilograms) of grass every day!

Baby bison eat grass in summer and sedges in winter.

The Koala

Koalas spend hours sitting in trees, chewing eucalyptus leaves. The poisonous leaves may make other animals sick. But they don't affect koalas at all!

This baby koala is learning from her mom how to choose the best eucalyptus leaves.

The Langur

This monkey lives in the tropical forests of Asia. Langurs sit in tree branches and munch on leaves, insects, fruit, and nuts. Sometimes they let their long tails dangle in the breeze.

A baby langur can hold on to tree branches with its feet or its tail while it eats.

Baby Canada geese use their short, wide beaks to pull up grass from the ground.

The Canada Goose

A little gosling may visit a farmer's field to peck away at corn and soybeans. The baby goose also eats plenty of grass and plants.

Yummy! Fruit and Nuts

Crunch, crunch! Hazelnuts, apples, grapes...
Squirrels, proboscis monkeys, and
porcupines love to munch on fruit and nuts!

The Proboscis Monkey

This funny-looking monkey is known for its giant nose! Proboscis monkeys like to eat fruit and leaves found in the forest. Despite their large size, these primates feel quite at home in the treetops.

Mom keeps a close eye on her baby as it tries different kinds of fruits.

The Squirrel

Squirrels love nuts and plants. This little rodent has sharp teeth that never stop growing! The squirrel's constant gnawing keeps its teeth from growing too long.

If you walk in the woods, maybe you will see a squirrel nibbling on acorns!

Porcupines have sharp, chisel-like teeth. They use them to munch on fruit.

The Porcupine

Porcupines look a little strange, all covered with sharp quills. These large rodents will eat almost anything that grows on trees, including leaves, twigs, nuts, bark, and berries.

Bohemian waxwings feed on small fruit that they pick with their beaks.

The Bohemian Waxwing

This magnificent bird lives in northern European forests. A chick's parents stuff it full of fruit until it is old enough to fly well. It will leave the nest when it is two to three weeks old.

Meat or Fish?

Some baby animals wait around for their parents to feed them meat or fish. Better hurry up...they are hungry!

The Pelican

A baby pelican sits up in the nest, waiting for its parents to return from fishing. It's no surprise that the youngster is anxious for their return. Pelicans eat several pounds of fish a day.

The baby pelican reaches into its parent's throat to eat pre-chewed mushy fish. Yum!

The Great Crested Grebe

Grebes take good care of their young. They feed them small fish that they catch by diving underwater.

Grebe parents take turns carrying their babies on their backs.

This wolf cub is eating tenderized meat. The adults in its pack have already chewed it!

The Wolf

Wolves are carnivorous predators. They hunt and kill other animals for food. The adults always share their prey with the wolf cubs in the pack. When returning from a hunt, each adult regurgitates pieces of meat to feed the hungry youngsters.

Insect Hunters

Although you might not be able to tell by looking at them, these animals are formidable hunters. Many baby animals quickly learn how to capture insects for food.

The Ladybug

Even though ladybug larvae are smaller than your fingernail, they eat like pigs! These larvae can wolf down dozens of aphids a day!

This ladybug larva is hunting aphids on flower stems.

The Bat-Eared Fox

This little fox with big ears lives on the African savanna. There it hunts termites and ants. It also eats beetles that it finds in the droppings of herbivores.

Shhh! With its snout to the ground, this young bat-eared fox is hunting for insects.

Chameleons use their long, sticky tongues to catch their prey.

The Chameleon

Chameleons have to feed themselves from the day they are born. Luckily, even babies know how to shoot out their tongues with amazing precision to capture insects. Very few get away!

The Chickadee

When chicks in their nest are hungry, they chirp for more food. Their parents bring them caterpillars, which they quickly devour. Soon, they will learn how to catch food themselves.

Baby chickadees usually swallow caterpillars without chewing them.

Killing Machine!

Would you believe this tiny masked bird is actually a fierce predator? Loggerhead shrikes feed their babies small animals they have killed.

That's Hard Work!

A male loggerhead shrike hunts all day to feed his hungry chicks. The little ones wait in the nest with their mother. She takes the food from the male to feed to the chicks.

Shrikes can kill animals as large as they are, such as shrews or frogs. Once they have their prey, they impale it on the thorns of a bush until they are ready to eat it.

Shrikes usually store their prey on thornbushes located close to their nests.

Baby shrikes in the nest open their beaks wide. Their parents stuff them full of insects and small pieces of meat.

Flowers on the Menu

How much do you know about honey possums, geckos, and hummingbirds? Because they eat flower nectar, they are called nectarivores.

The Réunion Island Day Gecko

These small lizards have no problem climbing up flower stems to get nectar. Their sticky feet enable them to cling to just about any surface.

These geckos live on Réunion Island in the Indian Ocean.

The Honey Possum

The honey possum is only about the size of your hand. It is found in Australia, where it lives in small bushes. Each morning, the honey possum goes out to gather nectar from flowers, using its long tongue.

Honey possums are so light, they can climb up flower stems without breaking them.

The Gray Langur

This primate's amazing stomach allows it to digest the large quantities of plants it eats each day. It can even prevent the poison in certain plants from making the langur sick!

Gray langurs live in trees in Asian forests. Animals that live primarily in trees are called arboreal.

The Hummingbird

This tiny bird beats its wings so fast that it can hover in place! The hummingbird uses its long tongue to sip flower nectar. It does not even have to land on any plants to eat.

Once they are able to fly, baby hummingbirds can gather nectar like their parents do.

The Bumblebee

Bzzzzzz...A bumblebee flies among the flowers. This busy insect is round with fuzzy yellow and black stripes. It eats flower nectar and gathers pollen on its feet to feed to its young.

Bumblebees are not aggressive toward humans, but sometimes they sting to defend themselves.

Hungry Brown Bear

Like pigs, badgers, and rats, brown bears are omnivorous. They eat just about anything—from insects to fish to plants.

Learn Your Lessons Well

Once a cub leaves the den where it was born, it will follow its mom around everywhere. She teaches the cub how to hunt insects, pick fruit, and catch fish. As the cub grows up, it will always know how to find food!

It's not easy catching fish! Cubs are not as coordinated as adult bears, but sometimes they manage to catch a salmon anyway.

Bears use their long claws to find food. This cub is hoping to find insects by digging in a rotted log.

There are not many nutrients in plants, so cubs must eat a lot of them to grow up big and strong.

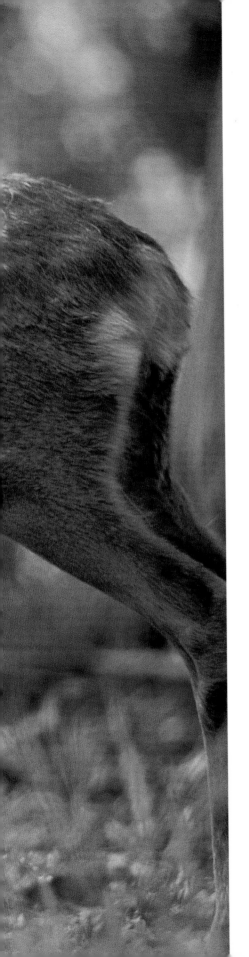

Happy to Be Me

Baby animals must stay healthy to grow up strong. They have to sleep enough, keep clean, and protect themselves from the weather.

All Clean!

You're not allowed to stay dirty in nature!
Did you know that many animals wash their
young to keep them from getting sick?

The Baboon

Calm has returned to the savanna. The baboons have stopped bickering. The parents sit on the ground to delouse their young. They're making sure that there are no lice in the babies' fur.

A female baboon uses her nails to remove the insects and dead skin from her baby's fur.

Only the female earwigs care for their eggs and larvae.

The Earwig

In the shelter of her burrow, a female earwig cleans her eggs. She uses her tongue to move the eggs around often so that they will not get moldy.

A mother hippopotamus invites her baby to take its first bath in the river with her.

The Hippopotamus

A baby hippo has very fragile skin. Its body produces a pink liquid to protect the youngster from the sun. But nothing feels better than a river bath when it comes to getting clean!

The Zebra

When zebras are with the herd, their striped coats trick predators. To clean themselves, zebra foals lick their backs and legs and use their teeth to detangle their fur.

Mom has to clean the body parts this foal can't reach.

Growing Up in the Cold

Animals can be found everywhere, including the coldest places on the planet! They grow up on the snow and ice—and in the water.

The Seal

Baby seals are called pups. They are born with a coat of thick white fur that protects them from the cold. The babies grow very fast, thanks to their mother's warm, fattening milk.

As it grows, this seal pup will lose its stunning white coat. Its skin will become as thick as its mother's.

The Emperor Penguin

This penguin lives at the South Pole—an icy region that is colder than a freezer. But babies are well protected. Their gray down acts like a big blanket, keeping them cozy and warm.

When it gets a little too cold, this penguin chick takes shelter under a parent's round, fluffy tummy.

Once they leave their den, these cubs will follow their mother to the frozen ocean.

The Polar Bear

Winter at the North Pole gets extremely cold. Polar bear cubs are able to survive because they are born in a sheltered den that their mother digs for them in the snow.

The Lemming

This rodent has long claws that it uses like a pickax to dig tunnels under the ice. When it gets too cold out, the lemming disappears into its shelter to sleep where it is warmer.

In winter, the lemming's coat becomes thicker to protect it from the cold.

Snuggled Up

In the mountains, baby groundhogs have a great way to withstand the cold weather. They hibernate—or sleep—in their burrows during winter.

In fall, groundhogs burrow into the dirt and create dens.

A Long Nap!

During winter, baby groundhogs live in slow motion. They sleep with their families deep in their burrows. Their hearts beat slowly and they almost seem like they are not breathing. They only wake up to go to the bathroom, then they go back to sleep until spring.

Winter is over and the groundhogs are back! They slept for a few months and then woke up. It is time to enjoy some yummy plants!

In summertime, baby groundhogs play outside their burrows. However, for the first two or three months, they never stray too far from their parents—the source of reassuring cuddles.

Life in the Desert

In sandy deserts, the weather is very hot and it hardly ever rains. However, some animals get by just fine in this difficult environment.

The Fennec

Fennec parents teach their babies how to keep cool by digging very deep dens in the sand. They stay in these dens all day and then go out at night to hunt insects, rodents, and reptiles.

Fennecs are also sometimes called desert foxes. They live in the Sahara.

The Sandgrouse

This bird lives in desert climates. Its plumage helps the sandgrouse blend in with its sandy surroundings. That makes it hard for predators to find it.

To give her chicks something to drink, the sandgrouse soaks her feathers in the pond. Her babies suck the water out of her feathers.

When it gets too hot, the oryx conserves
the water in its body by not sweating.

The Oryx

Oryx live in the deserts of Africa.
It rarely rains on these vast stretches
of sand. In order to survive in such
harsh conditions, these amazing
animals can go for weeks without
drinking a single drop of water.

Time for Bed

Zzzzzz...You've got to sleep to grow!
Baby animals sleep much more than their parents.

The Garden Dormouse

In fall, this little mammal settles into its burrow to hibernate. Once it gets too cold out, the dormouse will stop eating and go to sleep. It won't go out for another six or seven months.

Dormice sleep,
rolled up in little balls,
in birds' nests or barns.

The Ferret

Ferrets are nocturnal. They sleep for at least 18 hours a day. Sometimes they moan, move their tails, or move their feet when they are dreaming!

Baby ferrets from the
same litter sleep snuggled
up to each other.

The Barbary Ape

This monkey has powerful muscles and enormous canine teeth, but babies are very vulnerable. To avoid getting attacked, a baby always sleeps near its troop.

Resting on its mother's back, this baby feels totally safe.

The Pika

Pikas live in the mountains, where it is very cold. Sometimes they hide between large rocks to sleep. If a pika senses danger, it will wake up and emit a high-pitched whistle to alert its family.

This baby Ural owl is sleeping sitting up on a tree branch.

Pikas can sleep in just about any position.

The Ural Owl

This owl is a nocturnal raptor. It sleeps during the day and hunts at night. When the forest grows dark, the chick wiggles around in the nest—it is hungry.

Facing Danger

In nature, danger is always lurking nearby. When adults are not protecting them, baby animals must find a way to survive on their own.

Enemies Everywhere!

Baby animals are vulnerable and incapable of defending themselves. Other animals, called predators, watch their every move, hoping for a meal.

A cheetah carries its prey in its mouth as it looks for a shady spot to eat.

The Thomson's Gazelle

The gazelle's best defense against predators is to run away in a zigzag pattern. But this baby was too young. It could not yet run quickly enough to escape the fastest of the big cats.

The water bug has taken on a full-grown frog. It jabs its long beak into its prey to eat it.

The Tadpole

Not every tadpole will become a frog. The weakest get eaten by water bugs that hide among plants, waiting for their prey.

A toad would be easy prey for an adult ribbon snake. But for a baby snake, the roles are reversed. The toad is the predator.

The Ribbon Snake

When they are born, ribbon snakes are very thin and have a beautiful striped pattern. If threatened, the snake gives off an unpleasant odor but is not a danger to humans.

The Sea Lion

Sea lion pups swim more slowly than adults, and this great white shark knows it. Sea lions must be very careful of predators as they swim.

The white shark tosses the sea lion up in the air to knock it unconscious, then devours the pup in one bite.

Bodyguards

Sometimes adults must become bodyguards to protect their precious little ones. They would never leave their babies alone for even one second!

When wolves attack, musk oxen form a shield to protect their young.

The Musk Ox

These enormous arctic oxen are very strong and sport a pair of razor-sharp horns. Their main predators are wolves.

This baby opossum is trying to hang on to its mother's fur. It knows that is where it is the safest!

The Opossum

In the forest, a fox is prowling around baby opossums. They still have baby teeth and are too small to defend themselves. Luckily, their mother smelled danger and chased the predator away by growling.

When there is danger, rockhopper penguins defend their young by thrashing around as if to say, "Don't come any closer!"

The Rockhopper Penguin

With their funny feathers on their heads, these penguins always look like they got up on the wrong side of the bed! They can get very aggressive with rats, seagulls, or cats that threaten their chicks.

The European Stinkbug

There's only one way this mom can protect her many babies. She gets them all together on one leaf and watches over them until they are old enough to fend for themselves. Talk about a helicopter parent!

If her young are in danger, the European stinkbug furiously beats her wings to scare the enemy.

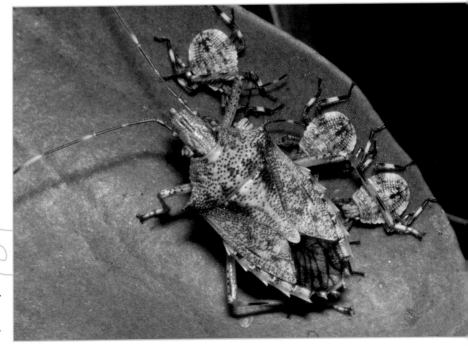

Safe from Danger

Many animals hide their babies—underground or behind rocks, for example—so predators can't find them.

The Prairie Dog

Although they do not live in trees, prairie dogs belong to the squirrel family. They have bushy tails and little pointed snouts. They live underground in tunnels that have several exits.

An eagle is approaching, so the prairie dogs race into their burrows.

The Shrew

Shrews often make their nests near homes. You've probably never seen one, though. They are very small—and careful to stay hidden. Shrews must always be wary of cats and birds that are watching and waiting to eat them.

This shrew family is going to find shelter. Look...they are walking in a single-file line!

This lioness is moving her cub to hide it. She carries it by the scruff of its neck.

The Lion

A lion might be the king of the beasts, but at birth, cubs are very weak. They can't see anything or stand up. They really need protection from adults to survive.

Not Seen, Not Eaten!

To avoid becoming lunch, some baby animals use camouflage to look like leaves, sticks, or rocks. Can you see them?

The Stick Insect

It looks like a twig! This thin, light insect looks so much like the plant it is on that it is almost impossible to see it! The insect is using mimicry.

Stick insects can sit on the same twig all day without moving.

The Hare

Baby hares are called leverets. They hide among dead leaves to sleep. But if a fox gets too close, the leveret quickly hops away.

This leveret is about the same size as a baby rabbit.

The Painted Frogfish

This bizarre fish can change shape and color in just a few hours. Each time it sits on sponges or coral, the frogfish changes to match its surroundings. You can't catch it if you can't find it!

The painted frogfish can turn yellow, red, or blue.

The Black-Backed Gull

Adult black-backed gulls lay their eggs on coastlines. After hatching, the chicks hide in the rocks. Their gray down makes them invisible to the cats that would love to eat them!

This fluffy ball is a young black-backed gull. It is about as big as your fist.

The Green Iguana

When they hatch from their eggs, you can see that baby iguanas are bright green! Since its skin is the same color as tree leaves, the iguana can rest without worrying about a snake or bird eating it.

When perfectly still, iguanas become invisible against the green foliage.

Clever Tricks

Some baby animals must learn to fend for themselves.
Since they are not very strong, they have to be clever.

The Armadillo

The bony plates covering an armadillo form a very hard shell that makes it look like a little dinosaur. Don't worry, though! This odd-looking animal is not dangerous at all. It only eats insects.

When a baby armadillo is frightened, it rolls up into a ball!

The Salamander

Salamanders live near rivers and ponds and only come out at night. They have poisonous skin. Their bright color is a warning to predators—one bite will make them sick.

When threatened, salamanders play dead and show their bright colors.

Watch out! The fins on this porcupine fish are venomous.

The Porcupine Fish

The porcupine fish's spines are usually folded against its body. But when it feels threatened, this fish breathes in water and puffs itself up. It becomes a huge, spiky ball that is impossible to swallow!

Pharaoh Eagle-Owl

When they leave the nest, baby owls are big enough to fly, but they are still vulnerable. They might be attacked while they are resting.

This young pharaoh eagle-owl ruffles its feathers to scare off enemies.

Hedgehog Tactics

Hedgehogs have as many as 5,000 quills on their backs!
They use the quills for protection when threatened.

Ouch! That's Prickly

At birth, baby hedgehogs' quills are hidden underneath their skin. But before long, hundreds of white spikes appear on their backs. Then baby hedgehogs look like big chestnuts!

Some hedgehogs make their nests in gardens. Their young are often hidden under piles of dead leaves.

This baby needs to be careful while walking in the grass. It could get attacked by a badger or a fox.

Like armadillos, baby hedgehogs protect themselves from danger by rolling up into balls.

Time for School

Like you, baby animals learn a lot of things as they grow up. If they want to survive on their own, most of them will need to know how to stay clean, hunt, or even fly.

3, 2, 1 . . . Go!

Baby animals are incapable of defending themselves. Predators watch their every move, hoping for a meal.

The Northern Gannet

If it wants to eat, first a gannet chick has to learn how to fish. It's okay if the fishing isn't good, though. When it gets big enough, this bird can go for a week without eating.

A northern gannet dives deep to catch fish. Getting it right is hard. A young gannet will make several unsuccessful attempts at first.

The Gazelle

To survive on the African savanna, young gazelles must know how to run fast. They quickly learn how to make impressive leaps to escape predators!

Even though this gazelle is just a baby, it can still run faster than any human!

This baby sea lion cannot swim fast enough to go into the ocean alone. Without its mom nearby, the pup could get attacked by an orca!

The Sea Lion

Just like its mom, a baby sea lion has everything it needs for swimming. It uses its flippers to move forward and its tail for steering underwater. However, the pup must mature a bit before it goes swimming alone.

The Black-Faced Cormorant

Baby cormorants are covered in black down. It protects them from the cold but doesn't allow them to fly. The birds can't leave the nest until their feathers grow in.

This young cormorant does not yet know how to fly. However, it is already practicing flapping its wings to develop its muscles.

Hunting Lessons

Most animals have to hunt for their food. As soon as they are old enough, young animals start learning from their parents how to capture prey.

The Orca

Orcas are also known as killer whales. Like its parents, a young orca will soon be an expert at hunting seals, sea lions, and other marine animals.

This mother orca is teaching her baby how to hunt in the cold ocean water.

The Cheetah

Young cheetahs can run very fast, but only for short distances. If they don't catch a gazelle on their first try, it will get away. It takes a lot of training to become a great hunter!

As soon as they are old enough, cheetahs go hunting with their mothers.

The Grizzly Bear

Each summer, millions of salmon invade northern rivers. And grizzly bears are waiting to catch them. It's a real feast!

Baby grizzlies do not yet know how to fish. Luckily, their mother will share the salmon she catches.

The Arctic Fox

Arctic foxes live where it is cold. They hunt rodents, birds, and fish. Sometimes they will follow a polar bear around to eat its leftover food.

This baby arctic fox will learn how to hunt by killing the birds its parents bring to it.

All Clean!

Young animals have to learn how to clean themselves from head to tail. Get to work, kids!

The Tiger

Tigers cannot hunt without their claws. These striped cats must be careful to always keep their claws clean so they won't get damaged.

This tiger is using its rough tongue like a washcloth.

The Brown Rat

This rat loves to keep clean! It washes itself from head to paw whenever it is dirty, cold, or just a little worried.

This baby brown rat is washing its cute little face with its paws.

The Fly

Once they are finished eating, flies wash themselves. They clean their legs and wings before flying away.

This fly is rubbing its legs together to remove grains of sugar that are stuck there.

The Diademed Amazon Parrot

These birds have pretty "handy" feet! They use them to hold on to branches or fruit and to remove seeds.

No manicure necessary! This parrot can care for its nails all by itself.

The Burrowing Owl

This owl has large feet and a small, spotted belly. It is active both day and night. The owl catches insects in the morning and hunts mammals at night.

Like all birds, the burrowing owl uses its beak to clean its feathers.

Grown-up Talk

As baby animals mature, so do their voices! When they are very little, babies' voices are often higher pitched and weaker than those of their parents.

The Wolf

Ahh-woooooo! Wolves howl to call to other wolves. Their family members respond immediately. The wolves' unique calls are an effective way of recognizing one another and communicating in the forest.

Wolf cubs have weaker voices than their parents. Each cub's voice has a different tone.

The Leopard

These cats live in the forests of Africa and Asia. They purr like big kitty cats. They can also roar to impress their enemies.

This baby leopard can't roar as loudly as its parents do.

Like their parents, baby howler monkeys have large throats. They will soon be able to yell a lot louder than you can!

The Howler Monkey

They are called howler monkeys because they are some of the loudest animals in tropical forests. Their calls are so loud that they can be heard from 3 miles (5 kilometers) away.

Homeschooling

Chimpanzees are the apes that most resemble humans. Baby chimpanzees live with their parents for many years—just like you.

It's not easy catching termites with a branch! Baby chimpanzees learn new skills by observing the adults in their group.

Life in the Forest

Baby chimps spend their nights snuggled up to their mother's warm body. During the day, the baby follows its mom around to each of her activities. She teaches it everything she knows.

Not all tree leaves are okay to eat. With its mom's help, this baby chimpanzee is learning to tell safe leaves from harmful ones.

Most apes do not know how to swim. Baby chimpanzees must be careful not to fall into a river. They could drown.

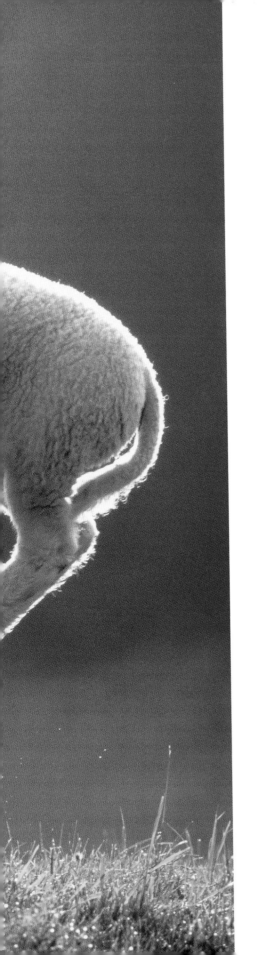

Yay for Play!

When they are not busy eating or *sleeping*, many baby animals spend their time playing and imitating the adults. What fun!

Everything Is Funny

No need for toys! Baby animals can have fun playing with each other and their parents—and develop their reflexes and muscles at the same time.

The Sheep

A lamb is the offspring of a ram and a ewe. When the youngster is with its flock, it likes to jump and play. Later it will be able to jump as well as the adults!

This little lamb is in a frisky mood!

The Lion

On the African savanna, lions live in family groups called prides. While the adults rest in the shade of acacia trees, the lion cubs play at chasing and biting one another.

This lion cub is pretending to "hunt" its mother's tail.

Baby macaques hang from tree branches to test their strength.

The Japanese Macaque

These monkeys have pinkish faces and thick fur. Many of them live on islands where the winters are very cold. The macaques grow up in the snow and take baths in hot springs.

The House Cat

Cats are small felines that chase birds and mice. However, until they reach one year old, kittens practice by catching flies, balls, or other toys.

Kittens love to tumble around for fun!

Fake Fighting

They might bite, shove, or hit one another, but don't worry.
Baby animals are only pretending to fight.

The Western Gray Kangaroo

Baby animals, like the gray kangaroo, play fight to practice for when they are older. Adult males fight over females for real!

Like the adults, these baby kangaroos are already using their tails to support them when they stand up.

The Alpine Ibex

These wild goats live in herds in the mountains. They are great climbers and are known for their long horns.

These young ibex are play fighting by butting their heads together.

The Warthog

This odd-looking animal lives on the African savanna. A warthog has warts on its head—which are actually protective bumps. It has sparse bristly hair on its body and a mane that runs down its back. Warthog mothers are very protective of their young.

These young warthogs are trying to push each other. The first one to stop pushing loses the game.

The Eurasian Lynx

These wild cats are great at hide-and-seek! They grow up well hidden in the forest and only leave their hiding places to hunt.

These young lynx play fight while their mother is away.

The Red Fox

A flash of red in the forest… Two fox kits are playing tag. Then they nip at each other as they pretend to fight. When they are older, they will have the skills they need to fight for real.

Who is the strongest? These young foxes are testing their strength while they build up their muscles.

A Very Playful Baby

What could this funny-looking nose be used for? While playing, elephant calves discover that they can do many things with their trunks.

A Strange Tool

An elephant uses its trunk to breathe, smell, touch, and communicate. This amazing appendage has thousands of tiny muscles. It is incredibly strong and long. And it weighs about four times as much as you do!

Elephant calves use their trunks to greet their friends.

An elephant calf learns very quickly how to use its trunk like a hand. This calf is using its trunk to pick corn.

Like most of its friends, this elephant calf loves to play in the river. It is fun to suck up water and then shower it down to get clean and refreshed.

All Grown Up!

Baby animals eventually grow up and leave their parents. Once they are adults, it is their turn to have babies!

Leaving the Group

When baby animals no longer need their family to feed and protect them, they go off and live on their own.

The Three-Toed Sloth

These animals are called sloths because *slothful* means "lazy." Sloths are among the slowest moving animals on the planet. Baby sloths are always with their mothers, hanging from tree branches. They only come down to go to the bathroom.

Sloths stay with their mothers for up to two years.

The Striped Skunk

Skunks spray a stinky liquid that smells worse than a stink bomb at anything or anyone that threatens them.

Striped skunks leave their mothers once they can defend themselves.

The Spotted Hyena

Hyenas have ears that stick out and sloping hindquarters. Their call sounds like a cruel laugh. Hyenas live in groups on the African savanna. They are skilled hunters that also scavenge other animals' kills.

Spotted hyenas grow up in burrows with their families. Females stay with their family group, but males go off on their own once they mature.

The Barracuda

When they are small, young barracudas stay together to avoid getting eaten by tuna. They form large groups, called schools. Then they separate from the group.

Some barracudas can grow to be twice your size!

The Humpback Whale

The humpback is named for the shape of its back when it dives under the water. These whales live alone or in small groups in oceans and seas all over the world.

Whale calves leave their moms once they are old enough to hunt for themselves.

A Difficult Separation

Orangutans are large, orangish apes that live in the rain forests of Sumatra and Borneo. Babies are raised by their moms and will stay with them for about seven years.

During the first weeks of its life, this scruffy little ape spends all day sleeping and drinking its mom's warm milk.

Weaning

In the Malay language, *orangutan* means "person of the forest." Like humans, baby orangutans are very close to their mothers, who feed them and keep them safe. Eventually mothers stop allowing their babies to drink their milk. This is called weaning.

While growing, baby orangutans eat fruit and leaves. Their moms may make them try more than 200 different plants!

Adult orangutans live alone, but from time to time, they meet up with their mothers again.

Becoming the Boss

You have to be very strong to lead a group...
and you will have to win some battles.

To show who is boss, this wolf bares his teeth. The other wolf lies down in submission.

The Wolf

Wolves live in groups called packs. Within this large family, wolf cubs must obey the two leaders in charge.

Young elk fight each other using their antlers to see who is stronger.

The Elk

Elk live in European and North American forests. Males can grow to weigh more than 700 pounds (318 kilograms) and have antlers as tall as you!

What a fight! At mealtimes, the most aggressive vultures eat first.

The Griffon Vulture

These large raptors nest in colonies in cliffs. They eat the bodies of dead cows or sheep that they find using their sharp eyesight as they soar high up in the sky.

The Mandrill

Mandrills can easily be recognized by what looks like war paint on their faces. This African monkey's bright colors appear around age six.

Would you believe that this ferocious look is actually a friendly gesture among mandrills?

Parents-to-Be

The baby animals are grown. The young males will now search for females to reproduce.

The Ruff

When this male is trying to impress a female, he displays his fancy plumage, or feathers. He tries to look attractive to show females that he is in good health and can make babies.

Male ruffs ruffle up their most beautiful feathers to attract females.

The Tree Frog

These pretty frogs live alone in forests. They have sticky pads on their feet that allow them to sit on or hop onto leaves without falling.

Ribbit! Ribbit! This male tree frog is croaking to let females know he is available.

Japanese cranes do a special dance before mating.

The Japanese Crane

These large black-and-white birds live in huge flocks in Asia. Males and females can reproduce when they are three or four years old.

The Grevy's Zebra

On the African savanna, the young zebras are getting restless. Males that are about six years old can make babies, so they fight to win over the female zebras.

This young zebra is rearing up in front of a female to show her how strong he is.

Index

Photo Credits